Empowered Habits is designed to be more than just a journal—it's a tool for intentional living, self-reflection, and personal growth. Over the next three months, you'll engage in daily practices that help you cultivate mindfulness, gratitude, and focus, allowing you to align your habits with your values and goals.

This journal invites you to begin each day with intention. By setting a clear purpose and tracking the habits that matter most, you'll find that even the smallest shifts can lead to significant transformation. Along the way, you'll also explore weekly quotes to inspire you and writing prompts to spark deeper self-reflection, keeping you grounded and motivated.

As you move through this journey, remember that growth is a process. Some days will be easier than others, but each moment of awareness brings you closer to living a life that feels authentically empowered. With that in mind, this journal isn't pre-dated so that if you skip a day, the page is never wasted. Remember, each day is an opportunity to begin again.

Let Empowered Habits be your companion as you navigate these next few months, building habits that not only support your goals but also empower you to live with greater clarity, gratitude, and purpose.

Here's to your growth!

River James Wood

fullbloomco.org

"And the day came when the risk to remain tight in a bud was more painful than the risk it took to blossom.

Life is a process of becoming, a combination of states we have to go through. Where people fail is that they wish to elect a state and remain in it. This is a kind of death.

Living never wore one out so much as the effort not to live.

Life is truly known only to those who suffer, lose, endure adversity and stumble from defeat to defeat.

Perfection is static, and I am in full progress.

-Anais Nin

Date: (today's date)

Intention: (I am statement i.e. I am patient)

Big Three: (Write to-do items in box, these are your *must* do's)

☐ ☐ ☐

Little Three: (Write to-do's next to checkbox—would be nice to get done)

☐

☐

☐

Mind & Body: (Write what you plan to do next to the check box—mind: meditation/reading body: exercise/movement)

☐

☐

Three Gratitudes: (Write inside box)

☐

Date:

Intention:

Big Three:

Little Three:

Mind & Body:

Three Gratitudes:

Date:

Intention:

Big Three:

Little Three:

Mind & Body:

Three Gratitudes:

Date:

Intention:

Big Three:

Little Three:

Mind & Body:

Three Gratitudes:

Date:

Intention:

Big Three:

☐ ☐ ☐

Little Three:

☐

☐

☐

Mind & Body:

☐

☐

Three Gratitudes:

Date:

Intention:

Big Three:

Little Three:

Mind & Body:

Three Gratitudes:

Date:

Intention:

Big Three:

Little Three:

Mind & Body:

Three Gratitudes:

Date:

Intention:

Big Three:

Little Three:

☐

☐

☐

Mind & Body:

☐

☐

Three Gratitudes:

Look back at the quote from Anais Nin from the beginning of this week. Which line stands out most to you? Choose one so-called "defeat" from your life to reflect on. How did this defeat impact you? What did you learn from it? How would you be different if it hadn't happened?

Notes:

"When you plant lettuce, if it does not grow well, you don't blame the lettuce. You look for reasons it is not doing well. It may need fertilizer, or more water, or less sun. You never blame the lettuce. Yet if we have problems with our friends or family, we blame the other person. But if we know how to take care of them, they will grow well, like the lettuce. Blaming has no positive effect at all, nor does trying to persuade using reason and argument. That is my experience. No blame, no reasoning, no argument, just understanding. If you understand, and you show that you understand, you can love, and the situation will change"
— **Thich Nhat Hanh**

Date:

Intention:

Big Three:

Little Three:

Mind & Body:

Three Gratitudes:

Date:

Intention:

Big Three:

Little Three:

Mind & Body:

Three Gratitudes:

Date:

Intention:

Big Three:

Little Three:

Mind & Body:

Three Gratitudes:

Date:

Intention:

Big Three:

Little Three:

Mind & Body:

Three Gratitudes:

Date:

Intention:

Big Three:

Little Three:

Mind & Body:

Three Gratitudes:

Date:

Intention:

Big Three:

Little Three:

Mind & Body:

Three Gratitudes:

Date:

Intention:

Big Three:

Little Three:

Mind & Body:

Three Gratitudes:

Look back at the quote by Thich Nhat Hanh from the beginning of this week. How does it make you feel? In what areas of your life are you carrying blame for yourself or others? How can you nurture yourself and others more deeply?

"Living the life that cries to be lived from the depth of our being frees up a lot of energy and vitality. The juices flow. Everyone around us benefits from the aliveness that we feel. On the other hand, suppressing that life, for whatever reason, takes a lot of our life energy just in the managing of the pretending."
— **Deborah Adele, The Yamas & Niyamas: Exploring Yoga's Ethical Practice**

Date:

Intention:

Big Three:

Little Three:

Mind & Body:

Three Gratitudes:

Intention:

Big Three:

Little Three:

Mind & Body:

Three Gratitudes:

Date:

Intention:

Big Three:

Little Three:

Mind & Body:

Three Gratitudes:

Date:

Intention:

Big Three:

Little Three:

Mind & Body:

Three Gratitudes:

Date:

Intention:

Big Three:

Little Three:

Mind & Body:

Three Gratitudes:

Date:

Intention:

Big Three:

Little Three:

Mind & Body:

Three Gratitudes:

Date:

Intention:

Big Three:

Little Three:

Mind & Body:

Three Gratitudes:

Look back at the quote by Deborah Adele from the beginning of this week. What parts of you are you suppressing? What life "cries to be lived from the depth of your being"? What is one thing you can do this week to live from those depths?

Notes:

"On one level, wisdom is nothing more profound than an ability to follow one's own advice."— **Sam Harris, Waking Up: A Guide to Spirituality Without Religion**

Date:

Intention:

Big Three:

Little Three:

Mind & Body:

Three Gratitudes:

Date:

Intention:

Big Three:

Little Three:

☐

☐

☐

Mind & Body:

☐

☐

Three Gratitudes:

Date:

Intention:

Big Three:

Little Three:

Mind & Body:

Three Gratitudes:

Date:

Intention:

Big Three:

Little Three:

Mind & Body:

Three Gratitudes:

Date:

Intention:

Big Three:

☐ ☐ ☐

Little Three:

☐

☐

☐

Mind & Body:

☐

☐

Three Gratitudes:

Date:

Intention:

Big Three:

Little Three:

Mind & Body:

Three Gratitudes:

Date:

Intention:

Big Three:

Little Three:

Mind & Body:

Three Gratitudes:

Look back at the quote by Sam Harris from the beginning of this week. What are three examples of advice that you have given to someone else, but aren't actively following? What steps would you need to take to honor the wisdom of your own advice?

Notes:

"The only way to become excellent is to be endlessly fascinated by doing the same thing over and over. You have to fall in love with boredom."

— James Clear, Atomic Habits: An Easy & Proven Way to Build Good Habits & Break Bad Ones

Date:

Intention:

Big Three:

Little Three:

Mind & Body:

Three Gratitudes:

Date:

Intention:

Big Three:

Little Three:

Mind & Body:

Three Gratitudes:

Date:

Intention:

Big Three:

Little Three:

Mind & Body:

Three Gratitudes:

Date:

Intention:

Big Three:

Little Three:

Mind & Body:

Three Gratitudes:

Date:

Intention:

Big Three:

Little Three:

Mind & Body:

Three Gratitudes:

Intention:

Big Three:

Little Three:

Mind & Body:

Three Gratitudes:

Date:

Intention:

Big Three:

Little Three:

Mind & Body:

Three Gratitudes:

Look back at the quote by James Clear from the beginning of this week. Choose three recurring "boring" tasks to examine. How can you become "fascinated" with those tasks? How can you add an element of play and curiosity to them?

Notes:

"We will learn that though we think big, we must act and live small in order to accomplish what we seek. Because we will be action and education focused, and forgo validation and status, our ambition will not be grandiose but iterative—one foot in front of the other, learning and growing and putting in the time."
— Ryan Holiday, Ego is the Enemy: The Fight to Master Our Greatest Opponent

Date:

Intention:

Big Three:

Little Three:

Mind & Body:

Three Gratitudes:

Date:

Intention:

Big Three:

Little Three:

Mind & Body:

Three Gratitudes:

Date:

Intention:

Big Three:

Little Three:

Mind & Body:

Three Gratitudes:

Date:

Intention:

Big Three:

Little Three:

Mind & Body:

Three Gratitudes:

Date:

Intention:

Big Three:

Little Three:

Mind & Body:

Three Gratitudes:

Date:

Intention:

Big Three:

Little Three:

Mind & Body:

Three Gratitudes:

Date:

Intention:

Big Three:

Little Three:

Mind & Body:

Three Gratitudes:

Look back at the quote by Ryan Holiday from the beginning of this week. Have you ever added something "small" to your routine that had a big impact? How did it make you feel? Do you still engage in that practice? What "small thing" can add to your routine now to help you achieve your goals?

Notes:

So, in an age of acceleration, nothing can be more exhilarating than going slow. And in an age of distraction, nothing is so luxurious as paying attention. And in an age of constant movement, nothing is so urgent as sitting still.

-Pico Iyer

Intention:

Big Three:

Little Three:

Mind & Body:

Three Gratitudes:

Date:

Intention:

Big Three:

Little Three:

Mind & Body:

Three Gratitudes:

Date:

Intention:

Big Three:

Little Three:

Mind & Body:

Three Gratitudes:

Date:

Intention:

Big Three:

Little Three:

Mind & Body:

Three Gratitudes:

Date:

Intention:

Big Three:

Little Three:

Mind & Body:

Three Gratitudes:

Date:

Intention:

Big Three:

Little Three:

Mind & Body:

Three Gratitudes:

Date:

Intention:

Big Three:

Little Three:

Mind & Body:

Three Gratitudes:

Look back at the quote by Pico Iyer from the beginning of this week. Do you agree with him? What does it feel in your body when you slow down? How does your heart feel in the stillness?

Notes:

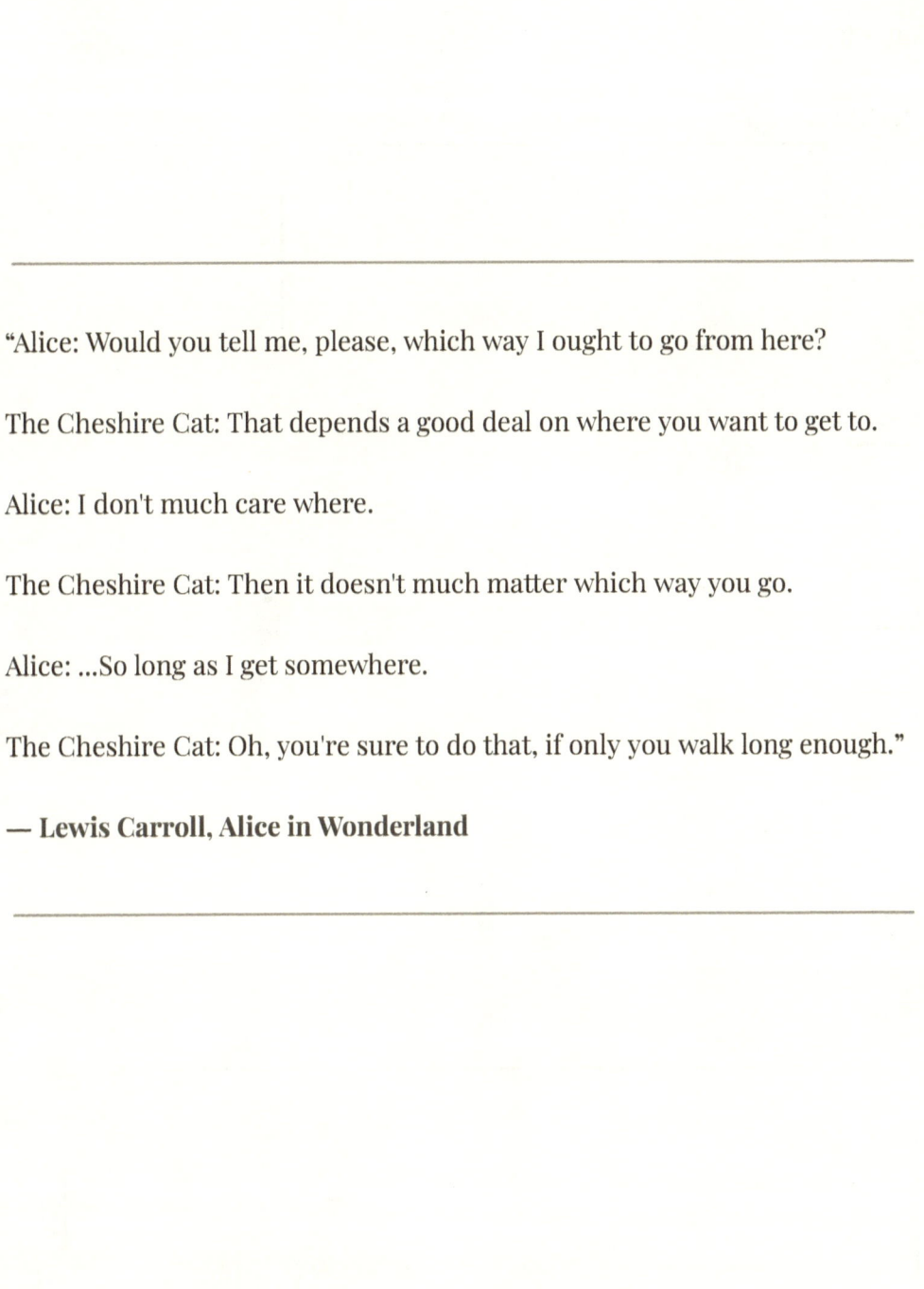

"Alice: Would you tell me, please, which way I ought to go from here?

The Cheshire Cat: That depends a good deal on where you want to get to.

Alice: I don't much care where.

The Cheshire Cat: Then it doesn't much matter which way you go.

Alice: ...So long as I get somewhere.

The Cheshire Cat: Oh, you're sure to do that, if only you walk long enough."

— **Lewis Carroll, Alice in Wonderland**

Date:

Intention:

Big Three:

Little Three:

Mind & Body:

Three Gratitudes:

Date:

Intention:

Big Three:

Little Three:

Mind & Body:

Three Gratitudes:

Date:

Intention:

Big Three:

Little Three:

Mind & Body:

Three Gratitudes:

Date:

Intention:

Big Three:

Little Three:

Mind & Body:

Three Gratitudes:

Date:

Intention:

Big Three:

Little Three:

Mind & Body:

Three Gratitudes:

Date:

Intention:

Big Three:

Little Three:

Mind & Body:

Three Gratitudes:

Date:

Intention:

Big Three:

Little Three:

Mind & Body:

Three Gratitudes:

Look back at the quote by the Cheshire Cat from the beginning of this week. When was the last time you set a long-term goal (the "destination" the Cheshire cat mentions)? Did you accomplish it? If you didn't, why not? If you did, what led to your success? Do you have another long-term goal in mind? What would it take for you to be ready to start that goal?

Notes:

I wish we had more respect for the great gift we are give, the silent hours, the interval of unknowing. Every night offer us a deep draft of the water of forgetfulness, the river Lethe, which we drink in remembrance of where we came from and in practice for our return. From it we rise renewed. Sleep is the strangest of initiations, the kindest of mysteries, a ceremony whose observance is blessing. I wish we held it in the honor and gratitude it deserves.

— Ursula K. Le Guin, Words Are My Matter

Date:

Intention:

Big Three:

☐ ☐ ☐

Little Three:

☐

☐

☐

Mind & Body:

☐

☐

Three Gratitudes:

Intention:

Big Three:

Little Three:

Mind & Body:

Three Gratitudes:

Date:

Intention:

Big Three:

Little Three:

Mind & Body:

Three Gratitudes:

Date:

Intention:

Big Three:

Little Three:

Mind & Body:

Three Gratitudes:

Date:

Intention:

Big Three:

☐   ☐   ☐

Little Three:

☐

☐

☐

Mind & Body:

☐

☐

Three Gratitudes:

Date:

Intention:

Big Three:

Little Three:

Mind & Body:

Three Gratitudes:

Date:

Intention:

Big Three:

Little Three:

Mind & Body:

Three Gratitudes:

Look back at the quote by Urusula K. Le Guin from the beginning of this week. What is your relationship with sleep? How many hours of sleep do you average a week? How do you feel when you wake up in the morning? How can you honor sleep as ceremony?

Notes:

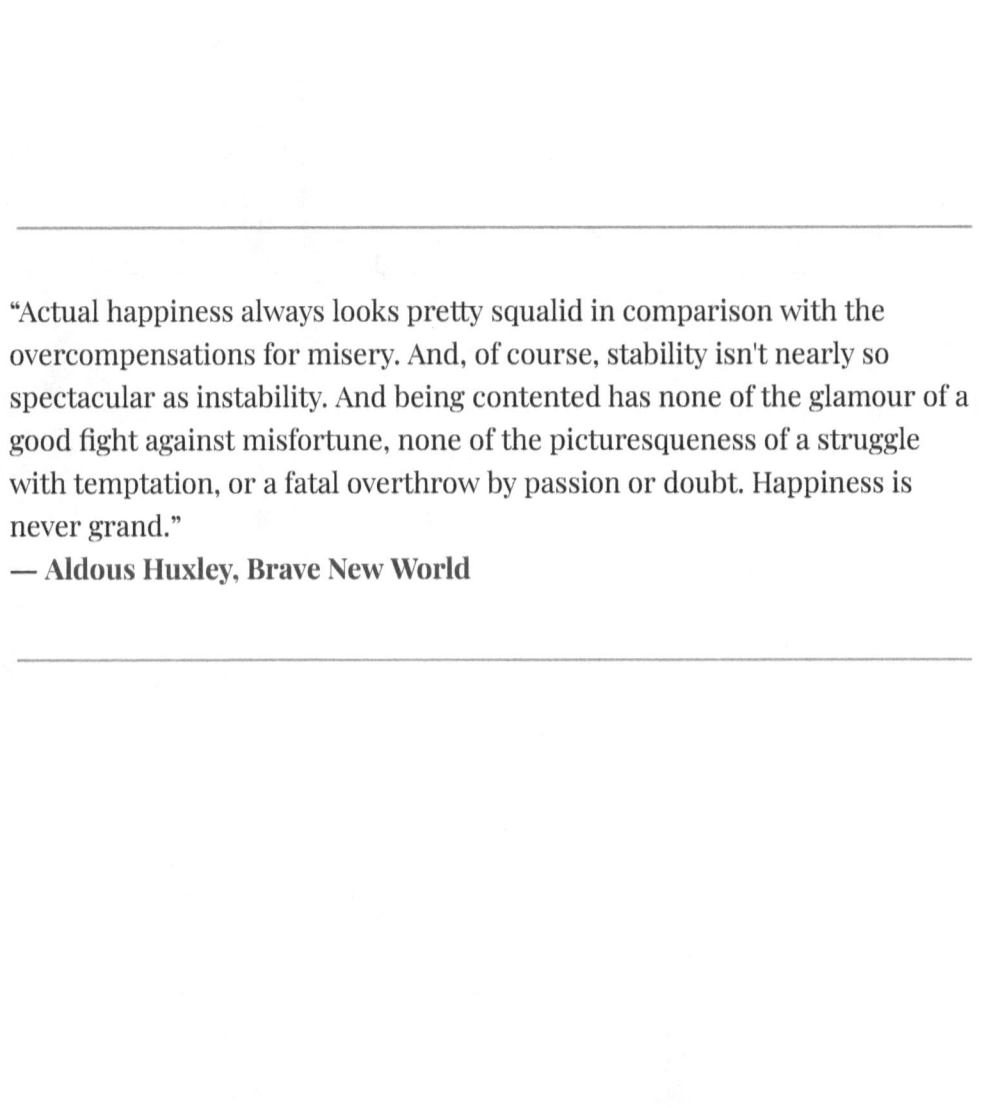

"Actual happiness always looks pretty squalid in comparison with the overcompensations for misery. And, of course, stability isn't nearly so spectacular as instability. And being contented has none of the glamour of a good fight against misfortune, none of the picturesqueness of a struggle with temptation, or a fatal overthrow by passion or doubt. Happiness is never grand."
— **Aldous Huxley, Brave New World**

Date:

Intention:

Big Three:

Little Three:

☐

☐

☐

Mind & Body:

☐

☐

Three Gratitudes:

Date:

Intention:

Big Three:

Little Three:

Mind & Body:

Three Gratitudes:

Date:

Intention:

Big Three:

Little Three:

Mind & Body:

Three Gratitudes:

Date:

Intention:

Big Three:

Little Three:

Mind & Body:

Three Gratitudes:

Date:

Intention:

Big Three:

Little Three:

Mind & Body:

Three Gratitudes:

Date:

Intention:

Big Three:

Little Three:

Mind & Body:

Three Gratitudes:

Date:

Intention:

Big Three:

Little Three:

Mind & Body:

Three Gratitudes:

Look back at the quote by Aldous Huxley from the beginning of this week. How do you feel about it? What areas of struggle in your life do you "glamourize"? What would it look like for you to be content?

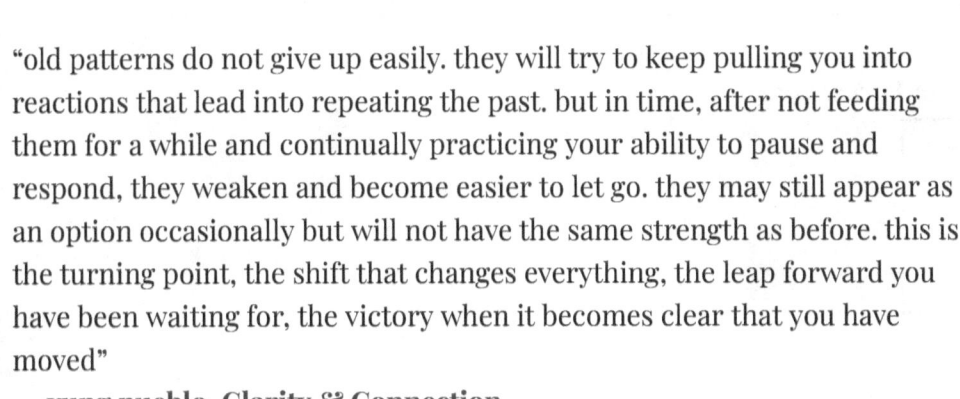

"old patterns do not give up easily. they will try to keep pulling you into reactions that lead into repeating the past. but in time, after not feeding them for a while and continually practicing your ability to pause and respond, they weaken and become easier to let go. they may still appear as an option occasionally but will not have the same strength as before. this is the turning point, the shift that changes everything, the leap forward you have been waiting for, the victory when it becomes clear that you have moved"

— **yung pueblo, Clarity & Connection**

Date:

Intention:

Big Three:

☐ ☐ ☐

Little Three:

☐

☐

☐

Mind & Body:

☐

☐

Three Gratitudes:

Date:

Intention:

Big Three:

Little Three:

Mind & Body:

Three Gratitudes:

Date:

Intention:

Big Three:

Little Three:

Mind & Body:

Three Gratitudes:

Date:

Intention:

Big Three:

Little Three:

Mind & Body:

Three Gratitudes:

Date:

Intention:

Big Three:

☐ ☐ ☐

Little Three:

☐

☐

☐

Mind & Body:

☐

☐

Three Gratitudes:

Date:

Intention:

Big Three:

Little Three:

Mind & Body:

Three Gratitudes:

Date:

Intention:

Big Three:

Little Three:

Mind & Body:

Three Gratitudes:

Look back at the quote by Yung Pueblo from the beginning of this week. What patterns in your life are no longer serving you? Write a list of these patterns, alongside their triggers. (ie: Pattern:Binge eating. Trigger: comments from my mother about my body). Now that you have identified the triggers, write a NEW list with the trigger alongside your *desired* pattern. (ie: Trigger: comments from my mother about my body. Pattern: call a trusted friend to vent).

"Not the world, not what's outside of us, but what we hold inside traps us. We may not be responsible for the world that created our minds, but we can take responsibility for the mind with which we create our world."
— **Gabor Maté, In the Realm of Hungry Ghosts: Close Encounters with Addiction**

Date:

Intention:

Big Three:

Little Three:

Mind & Body:

Three Gratitudes:

Date:

Intention:

Big Three:

Little Three:

Mind & Body:

Three Gratitudes:

Date:

Intention:

Big Three:

Little Three:

Mind & Body:

Three Gratitudes:

Date:

Intention:

Big Three:

Little Three:

Mind & Body:

Three Gratitudes:

Date:

Intention:

Big Three:

Little Three:

Mind & Body:

Three Gratitudes:

Date:

Intention:

Big Three:

Little Three:

Mind & Body:

Three Gratitudes:

Date:

Intention:

Big Three:

Little Three:

Mind & Body:

Three Gratitudes:

Look back at the quote by Gabor Mate from the beginning of this week. In what ways do you feel trapped by the world? How can you look at these feelings differently? Do you believe that you create your own world?

Notes:

"Life isn't about finding yourself, it's about creating yourself."
— **George Bernard Shaw**

Date:

Intention:

Big Three:

Little Three:

Mind & Body:

Three Gratitudes:

Date:

Intention:

Big Three:

Little Three:

Mind & Body:

Three Gratitudes:

Date:

Intention:

Big Three:

Little Three:

Mind & Body:

Three Gratitudes:

Date:

Intention:

Big Three:

☐ ☐ ☐

Little Three:

☐

☐

☐

Mind & Body:

☐

☐

Three Gratitudes:

Date:

Intention:

Big Three:

Little Three:

Mind & Body:

Three Gratitudes:

Date:

Intention:

Big Three:

☐ ☐ ☐

Little Three:

☐

☐

☐

Mind & Body:

☐
☐

Three Gratitudes:

Date:

Intention:

Big Three:

☐ ☐ ☐

Little Three:

☐

☐

☐

Mind & Body:

☐

☐

Three Gratitudes:

Look back at the quote by George Bernard Shaw from the beginning of this week. Who are you? Who do you want to be? Over the last three months, as you've committed to these habits, how have you changed?

Notes: